BASEBALL

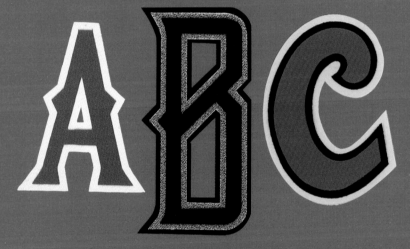

Florence Cassen Mayers

Harry N. Abrams, Inc., Publishers
An Official Publication of
Major League Baseball

For my daughters, Lela and Dara,
and my husband, Bob

With special thanks to Jeffrey Hoffeld,
Michael Mayers, and John, Anthony, and Nick Schiff

Editor: Sharon AvRutick
Designer: Florence Cassen Mayers
Photo Research: Bonnie E. Powers

Library of Congress Cataloging-in-Publication Data
Mayers, Florence Cassen.
Baseball ABC / by Florence Cassen Mayers.
p.   cm.
ISBN 0–8109–1938–9
1. Baseball—Juvenile literature.   [1. Baseball—Miscellanea.
2. Alphabet.]   I. Title.
GV867.5.M387   1994
796.357—dc20   94–1167

Published in 1994 by Harry N. Abrams, Incorporated, New York
A Times Mirror Company

Printed and bound in Hong Kong

Front Cover
A: Pittsburgh Pirates
B: Atlanta Braves
C: Colorado Rockies

Title Page
A: Texas Rangers
B: Milwaukee Brewers
C: Cleveland Indians

Introduction

This ABC is for baseball fans of all ages. In these pages you'll find photographs that capture the thrill of America's national game; you'll meet some of baseball's greatest players; and you'll see team pennants, caps, and jerseys, both old and new. From A for autograph to K for knuckleball to T for ticket and trophy, each letter gives you a bit of vital information about baseball history, tradition, or equipment. Brilliant full-color photos introduce the young child to our national pastime as well as to the alphabet. Older kids and their parents will cheer this generous collection of baseball memorabilia, paraphernalia, and action-packed game shots. This book is your ticket, peanuts, popcorn, and Cracker Jacks, your box seat at the big game.

F.C.M.

Babe Ruth was the first of twenty players to sign this page
of the American All-Star Tour of Japan photo album in 1934.

World Champions in 1950,
the New York Yankees
autographed this baseball.

Ted Williams wrote his name across the sweet spot of this ball in 1955, when he hit .356. With a .406 batting average in 1941, Williams was the last player to hit over .400.

Ted Williams

A
Pittsburgh Pirates

Autograph

A a

Houston Astros

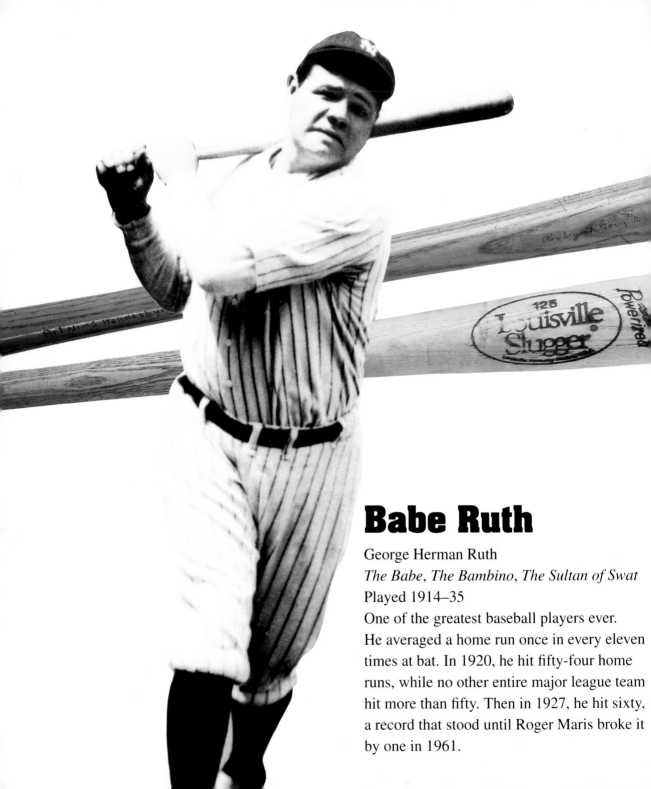

Babe Ruth

George Herman Ruth
The Babe, *The Bambino*, *The Sultan of Swat*
Played 1914–35
One of the greatest baseball players ever.
He averaged a home run once in every eleven
times at bat. In 1920, he hit fifty-four home
runs, while no other entire major league team
hit more than fifty. Then in 1927, he hit sixty,
a record that stood until Roger Maris broke it
by one in 1961.

With this bat, Lou Gehrig won the Triple Crown in 1934 with a .363 batting average, 49 home runs, and 165 RBI.

Don Mattingly used this bat to tie a major league record in 1987, hitting a home run in eight consecutive games.

Bat

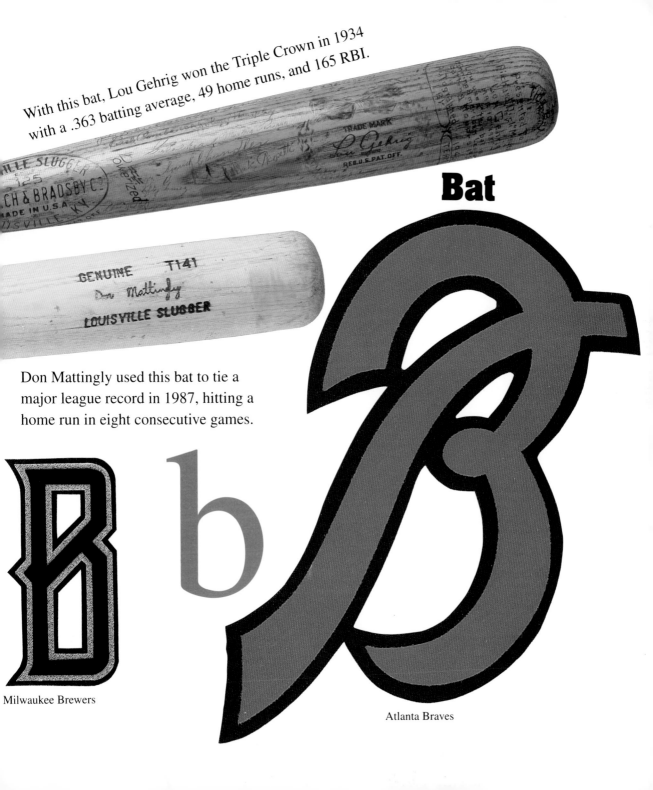

b

Milwaukee Brewers

Atlanta Braves

Cap

Caps like those used today date back to the early days of baseball. On one early team, players wore different color caps to designate their positions. Today, of course, specific colors—and logos—represent different teams. Here you see the caps of seven American League teams. (You will find the other seven teams later in this book.)

Chicago Cubs

WAGNER, PITTSBURG

Card

In 1991, this very rare Honus Wagner card sold for $451,000, the highest price paid for a baseball card to date. Very few of these cards exist today since Wagner, objecting to their being sold with tobacco, withdrew them soon after they were printed.

Detroit Tigers

Diamond

The field where the game is played. Soon after Alexander Cartwright laid out the first regulation baseball field in 1845, the term *diamond* was born. This is Joe Robbie Stadium, Miami.

e

E

E

Error

Even a superstar can make
an error, as Rickey Henderson,
who has stolen more bases
than anyone in major league
history, showed when he
dropped this fly ball in the
1992 American League
Championship Series.

f

F

Fan

The ballpark is filled with crowds whose love of the game begins at enthusiastic and ends at fanatic. An all-time single-team attendance record was set in 1993, when the Colorado Rockies attracted nearly 4.5 million fans.

Fielder

First baseman

San Francisco Giants

g

Texas Rangers

Fielder

Fielder

Catcher

First baseman

Catcher

Glove

Made of leather, a glove protects the hand and helps the player catch the ball. Early gloves were smaller than those used today. Catchers, first basemen, and fielders wear gloves designed for the needs of their different positions.

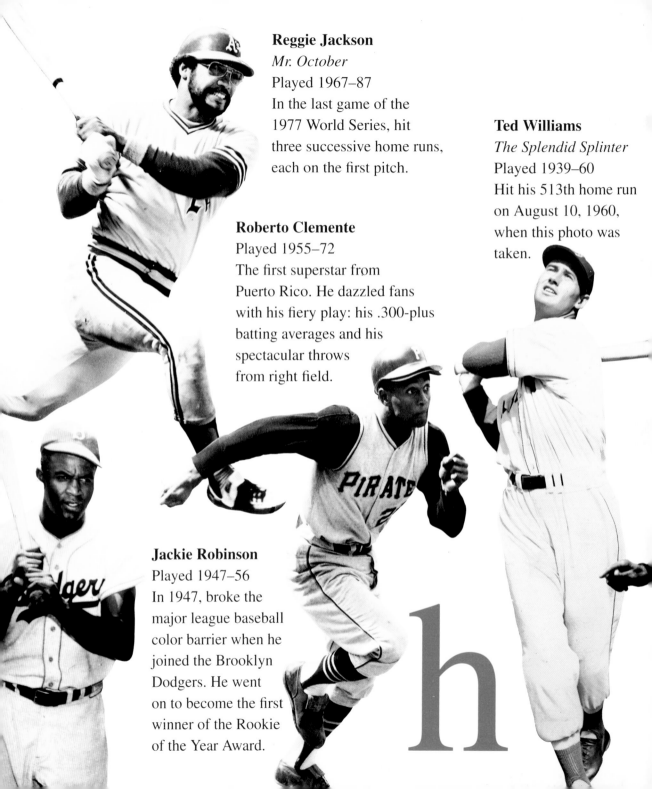

Reggie Jackson
Mr. October
Played 1967–87
In the last game of the 1977 World Series, hit three successive home runs, each on the first pitch.

Ted Williams
The Splendid Splinter
Played 1939–60
Hit his 513th home run on August 10, 1960, when this photo was taken.

Roberto Clemente
Played 1955–72
The first superstar from Puerto Rico. He dazzled fans with his fiery play: his .300-plus batting averages and his spectacular throws from right field.

Jackie Robinson
Played 1947–56
In 1947, broke the major league baseball color barrier when he joined the Brooklyn Dodgers. He went on to become the first winner of the Rookie of the Year Award.

h

Hero

Houston Astros

Joe DiMaggio
The Yankee Clipper
Played 1936–51
Hit safely in fifty-six consecutive games in 1941. No one else has approached that record in the major leagues.

Mickey Mantle
The Mick
Played 1951–68
Clouter of colossal home runs. In 1956, he won the Triple Crown: He led the league with 52 home runs, 130 runs batted in, and a .353 batting average.

Willie Mays
Say Hey Kid
Played 1951–73
Beloved for more than two decades for his consistent slugging, great center-field play, and the joy he brought to the game every single day.

Hank Aaron
Hammerin' Hank
Played 1954–76
Set the lifetime record for home runs, 755, surpassing Babe Ruth's 714.

The perfect geometry of a baseball infield is apparent in this view of Milwaukee's County Stadium: It's ninety feet from one base to the next, and sixty feet, six inches from the pitching rubber to home plate.

Infield

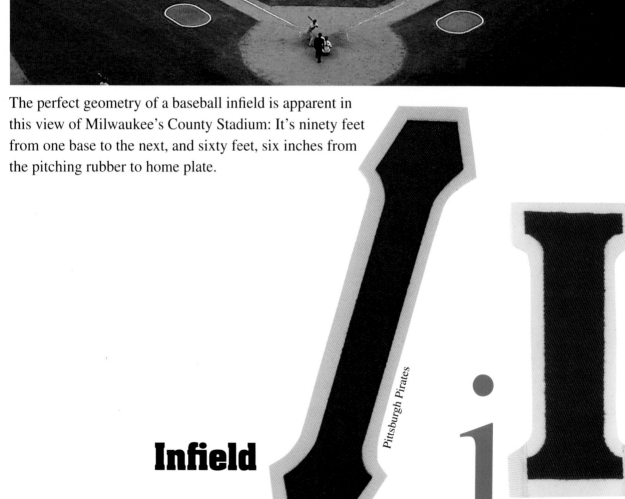

Pittsburgh Pirates

Colorado Rockies

j

J

Toronto Blue Jays

Jersey

Teams wear different jerseys when they practice, when
they play at home, and when they're on the road. At home,
the Reds wear the jersey with their logo, and when they're
on the road, they wear the one that says "Cincinnati."

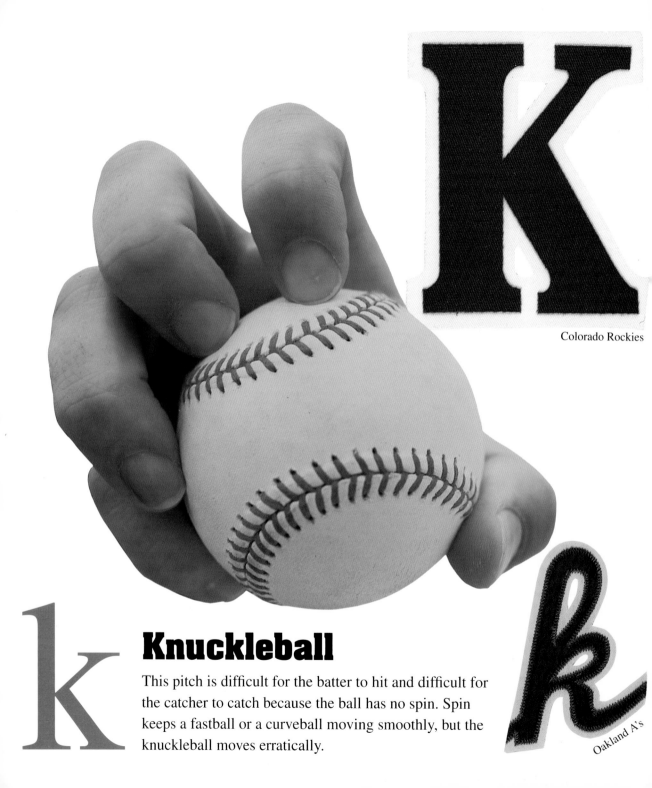

Colorado Rockies

Knuckleball

This pitch is difficult for the batter to hit and difficult for the catcher to catch because the ball has no spin. Spin keeps a fastball or a curveball moving smoothly, but the knuckleball moves erratically.

Oakland A's

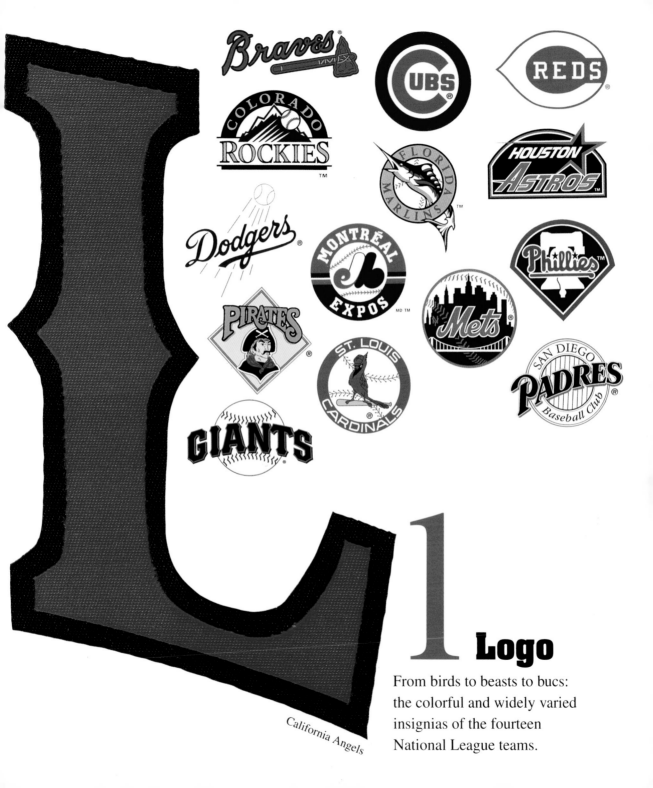

California Angels

1 Logo

From birds to beasts to bucs:
the colorful and widely varied
insignias of the fourteen
National League teams.

Catchers wear masks to protect their faces and necks. Early ones resembled simple bird cages, but they evolved into today's more elaborate, high-tech models.

Seattle Mariners

1890

1895

1915

Mask

1993 Boston Red Sox

Boston Red Sox

N

Night game

The first major league night game ever
was played on May 24, 1935, at Crosley Field
in Cincinnati. This is a blimp's-eye view of
Veterans Stadium, Philadelphia, at night.

n

Baltimore Orioles

Oakland A's

Out

"Yer OUT!" A home plate umpire calls a batter out on a third strike.

Philadelphia Phillies

Pp

Pennant

Pennants—along with bats, caps, and programs—are among the most-loved souvenirs collected by fans of every ballclub.

Pine tar

Batters put this sticky stuff on the bat to secure their grip. According to the rules, you can put it no more than eighteen inches up from the end of the bat handle.

RED SOX
BOSTON RED SOX
BOSTON

YANKEES
NEW YORK

ORIOLES
Orioles BALTIMORE
BALTIMORE

KANSAS CITY ROYALS
Royals

TWINS
MINNESOTA Twins
MINNESOTA

WHITE SOX
CHICAGO

DETROIT TIGERS
DETROIT TIGERS

PINE TAR
DANGER
HARMFUL OR FATAL IF SWALLOWED
NET CONTENTS 1 QT. (.946 ML)

"It ain't over 'til it's over."
—*Yogi Berra*

Quote

"The secret of managing is to keep the guys who hate you away from the guys who are undecided."
— *Casey Stengel*

"The other teams could make trouble for us if they win."
—*Yogi Berra*

"Let's play two."
— *Ernie Banks*

"The Yankees don't pay me to win every day, just two out of three."
— *Casey Stengel*

"Nice guys finish last."
—*Leo Durocher*

San Diego Padres

R

Seattle Mariners

R

r

Kansas City Royals

R

Runner

The runner racing to steal a base while the catcher hurls the ball is one of the most exciting plays in baseball. Base stealing has been around since the beginning of the game. In 1993, Kenny Lofton of the Cleveland Indians led the major leagues in stolen bases.

Safe

The umpire signals "safe" as the runner slides into home before the catcher makes the tag.

California Angels

Spikes

This pair belonged to fleet-footed center fielder Willie Mays, who led the league in stolen bases four times.

t

Minnesota Twins

Trophy

This is what it's all about: the World Series trophy.

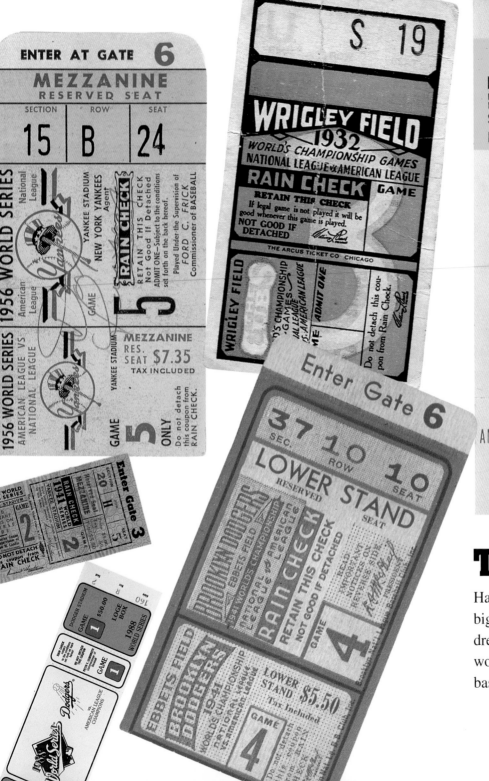

ENTER AT GATE **6**

MEZZANINE
RESERVED SEAT

SECTION	ROW	SEAT
15	B	24

1956 WORLD SERIES
National League

Yankee Stadium
New York Yankees

RAIN CHECK
RETAIN THIS CHECK
Not Good If Detached
ADMIT ONE—Subject to the conditions
set forth on the back hereof.

FORD C. FRICK
Commissioner of BASEBALL

GAME **5**

1956 WORLD SERIES
AMERICAN LEAGUE vs.
NATIONAL LEAGUE

Yankee Stadium

MEZZANINE
RES.
SEAT $7.35
TAX INCLUDED

GAME **5** ONLY

Do not detach
this coupon from
RAIN CHECK.

S 19

WRIGLEY FIELD
1932
WORLD'S CHAMPIONSHIP GAMES
NATIONAL LEAGUE vs AMERICAN LEAGUE

RAIN CHECK GAME

RETAIN THIS CHECK
If legal game is not played it will be
good whenever this game is played.
**NOT GOOD IF
DETACHED**

THE ARCUS TICKET CO CHICAGO

ADMIT ONE

Do not detach this cou-
pon from Rain Check.

AISLE	BOX	SEAT
43/49 AA		26

1977 WORLD SERIES

FIELD BOX
PARK IN ANY ODD
NUMBERED YELLOW LOT
$15.00

DODGER STADIUM

ADMIT
ONE

GAME **5**

**1977
WORLD
SERIES**

Dodgers ®

VS.
AMERICAN LEAGUE CHAMPION

RAIN CHECK subject to the conditions set forth on back hereof.
DO NOT DETACH THIS COUPON

BOWIE K. KUHN,
Commissioner of Baseball

GAM

5

Enter Gate **6**

SEC.	ROW	SEAT
37	10	10

LOWER STAND
RESERVED SEAT

BROOKLYN DODGERS
EBBETS FIELD

RAIN CHECK
RETAIN THIS CHECK
NOT GOOD IF DETACHED

GAME **4**

EBBETS FIELD
BROOKLYN DODGERS
1941
WORLD'S CHAMPIONSHIP
NATIONAL LEAGUE
vs. AMERICAN LEAGUE

LOWER
STAND $5.50
Tax Included

GAME **4**

Section
20
Reserved Seat
MEZZANINE
1941 WORLD SERIES

RAIN CHECK

Enter Gate **3**

GAME **2**

GAME **2**

Yankee Stadium

DO NOT DETACH
this coupon from
RAIN CHECK

DODGER STADIUM

$50.00

LOGE
BOX

160

GAME **1**

1988
WORLD SERIES

GAME **1**

World Series
VS.
AMERICAN LEAGUE
CHAMPIONS

Dodgers

Ticket

Having a ticket to a
big game is every fan's
dream, the passport to a
world of indelible
baseball memories.

u

Toronto Blue Jays

Umpire

During the regular season, there are
four umpires, one at each base. In the
World Series, two more are added,
one down each foul line.

Vendor

V

V

"Get your hotdogspopcornpeanutscrackerjacksodaicecoldbeer," he shouts as he makes his way through the stands.

W

Windup

Left-handed pitcher
Mark Langston
takes a full windup.
He raises his right
foot high in the air
(the kick), sets it
(the plant), and
finally throws the
ball (the delivery).

Cuban X-Giants

When African-American players were not permitted to play in the major leagues, they formed teams—and, later, leagues—the only place they could earn a living playing until the game was integrated in 1947. Some of the greatest athletes of all time were confined to the Negro Leagues for their entire careers. The Cuban X-Giants played in the first decade of this century.

Boston Red Sox

X

Yearbook

These annuals preview the upcoming season and celebrate and summarize the past with photographs, statistics, and biographies of players, managers, umpires, and coaches.

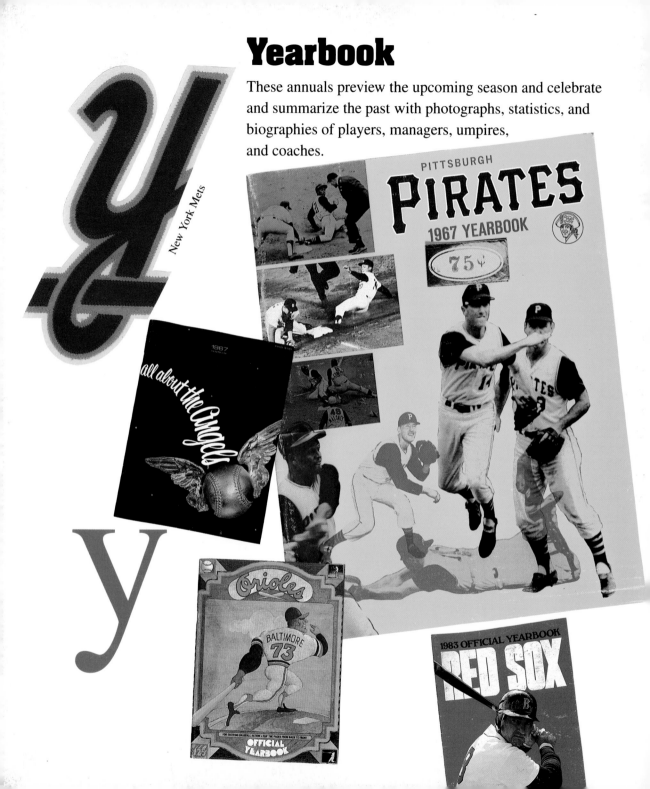

New York Mets

PITTSBURGH PIRATES
1967 YEARBOOK
75¢

1967

all about the Angels

Orioles

BALTIMORE
73

OFFICIAL YEARBOOK

1983 OFFICIAL YEARBOOK
RED SOX

Z

Zero

Z

How many zeros can you find on this scoreboard? In baseball, "goose egg" is another term for zero.

Photograph Credits

Introduction: photograph Rick Muller. A: book page courtesy
Richard Wolffers Auctions, San Francisco; ball (left) courtesy
Leland's Auction House; ball (right) courtesy Richard Wolffers
Auctions, San Francisco. B: photograph of Babe Ruth reproduced
with permission of Curtis Management Group; bats courtesy
Cowen Media/photograph Richard Walker. C: caps courtesy New
Era Company, Inc./photograph Rick Muller; Honus Wagner card
courtesy Richard Wolffers Auctions, San Francisco. D: photo-
graph Tom DiPace/MLB Photos. E: photograph courtesy *The
Sporting News.* F: photograph David Lilienstein. G: old gloves
photograph Richard Walker; new gloves courtesy Wilson Sporting
Goods/photograph Rick Muller. H: photographs courtesy *The
Sporting News.* I: photograph Ron Vesely/MLB Photos. J: jerseys
courtesy Russell Athletic/photograph Rick Muller. K: photograph
Jon SooHoo, courtesy Los Angeles Dodgers. L: photograph Rick
Muller. M: old masks photograph Richard Walker; new mask
courtesy All-Star Sporting Goods/photograph Rick Muller.
N: photograph David Lilienstein. O: photograph Stephen Green.
P: pine tar courtesy Hillerich & Bradsby; pennants courtesy Win-
Craft/photograph Rick Muller. R: photograph David Liam Kyle,
courtesy System 4 Ltd. S: spikes photograph Richard Walker; safe
photograph Stephen Green. T: trophy photograph Johan Sorensen,
courtesy System 4 Ltd.; tickets photographs Richard Walker.
U: photograph Stephen Green. V: photograph Jay Maisel.
W: photographs Mickey Palmer/MLB Photos. X: photograph
courtesy Negro Leagues Baseball Museum; cap courtesy Coop-
erstown Ball Cap/photograph Rick Muller. Y: photographs
Richard Walker. Z: photograph Stephen Green. Letters from team
jerseys courtesy Liebe.